Clayton Kershaw

Pitching Ace

SportStars
Volume 4

Clayton Kershaw

Pitching Ace

SportStars
Volume 4

A Biography By
Christine Dzidrums

CREATIVE MEDIA, INC.
PO Box 6270
Whittier, California 90609-6270
United States of America

The publisher does not have any control and does not assume any
responsibility for author or third-party website or their content.

www.CreativeMedia.net

Cover and Book design by Joseph Dzidrums
Cover photo by Joseph Dzidrums

First Edition: March 2014

Library of Congress Control Number: 2013912515

ISBN 978-1-938438-32-5   10 9 8 7 6 5 4 3 2 1

To Mom,

The Most Loyal Dodger Fan I Know

Table of Contents

"I hope baseball is a part of my legacy, but just a small part."

Chapter One

Clayton Edward Kershaw was born on March 19, 1988, in Dallas, Texas. Several months after the boy's birth, the Los Angeles Dodgers won the World Series in memorable fashion. Pitching sensation Orel Hershiser ultimately snagged the Most Valuable Player Award for his remarkable season in Los Angeles. Major League Baseball's legendary team would wait twenty long years before they would find another dominant starting pitcher. The player's name? Clayton Kershaw.

Clayton's dad, Christopher, was a remarkable musical talent. The gifted composer earned a modest living by writing advertising jingles. For his outstanding efforts, he received a CLIO Award, advertising's most prestigious honor.

Clayton's mom, Marianne, was a devoted parent who described her son's birth as the happiest day of her life. From day one, she had a deep bond with her only child. The caring mother would play an integral role in her son's life even when he reached adulthood.

Deeply religious, the Kershaws attended church services every Sunday morning to express appreciation for their many blessings. Clayton learned at an early age the importance of helping less-fortunate people. The charitable trait would remain with him for the rest of his life.

Like many children, Clayton loved sports, particularly baseball. The active youngster spent many hot afternoons under the Texas sun playing catching with family and friends. When he tired of playing outdoors, the baseball fan would head inside and watch a televised game. His favorite player was first baseman Will Clark. The six-time All Star, who played for the Texas Rangers from 1994-1998, boasted stellar hitting skills and exceptional fielding abilities.

Eventually, Clayton joined a Little League Baseball team. Like most young ballplayers, he loved taking batting practice. Yet, the talented athlete discovered that he also excelled at throwing a baseball, displaying great force and pinpoint precision.

Dallas, TX

Clayton Edward Kershaw
PR Photos

Excited by Clayton's natural gift, coaches transformed the phenom into a pitcher. The youth made a smooth transition into his new, challenging role. In fact, he even acquired a curveball by the age of eight!

A conscientious player, Clayton strove to improve his pitching fundamentals. He studied Major League pitchers carefully and emulated their techniques. He especially admired the pitching mechanics of Johan Santana, an All-Star ace for the Minnesota Twins and later the New York Mets. Twice in his career, Johan had captured the Cy Young Award, Major League Baseball's top pitching honor.

Ready For Flight
Glenn Harris - PR Photos

Bursting with energy, Clayton rarely slowed down when he left the baseball diamond. The versatile athlete split his time between youth football and soccer leagues. For many years, he juggled three sports!

While playing on one particular soccer team, Clayton became friends with a youngster named Matthew Stafford, an exceptional athlete who would one day become the Detroit Lions' star NFL quarterback. The two boys became great friends and hung out at one another's house all the time. They even invented a game called Hallway Hockey, an indoor two-person version of the sport.

Clayton's reputation at school mirrored his stature on the playing field. He was an eager learner with an admirable work ethic. His even-tempered, polite personality made him popular with classmates and teachers.

Shortly after Clayton turned ten years old, his easygoing life hit its first speed bump. His mother and father filed for a divorce. Although his parents no longer lived together, his dad found an apartment nearby.

Throughout the changes in Clayton's home life, baseball remained his constant passion. In four years' times, he would begin classes at Highland Park High, a reputable school with strict academic standards and a renowned athletic department. The young talent couldn't wait to pitch for the school that *Sports Illustrated* had lauded for having the best sports program in all of Texas!

"I'm not worried when I pitch. I just want to get ready and do the best I can."

Chapter Two

While attending classes at Highland Park High, Clayton juggled academic courses with after-school sports. In the fall of 1996, the fourteen-year-old made the football team playing center, while Matthew guided the team as quarterback. Strangely enough, despite leading an active life, the teenager battled weight issues.

"When I was a freshman, I was short and fat," he later told *Baseball America*. "I just grew and started working out. It's funny to think about how far physically I've come from freshman year."

Hoping to improve his skills on the mound, Clayton also played for The Dallas Baseball Academy of Texas, an institution that prides itself on teaching young ballplayers the sport's correct fundamentals. While at the academy, Clayton took pitching lessons from Skip Johnson, a well-respected baseball instructor. The diligent athlete soon saw a significant improvement in his breaking ball pitch.

As Clayton's pitching blossomed, people praised his athletic ability. More importantly, the youngster worked hard and showed respect toward his coaches. His combination of natural talent and dedication to work hard would bode well for his promising future.

Off the field, Clayton enjoyed a thriving social life. The star pitcher began dating a classmate named Ellen Melson. He had known the pretty brunette since middle school and considered her a girlfriend and best friend.

By Clayton's senior year of high school, baseball experts viewed him as one of the country's top prospects. The phenom finished his final season with a 13-0 record, 0.77 ERA and 139 strikeouts in 64 innings. He even set Highland Park's school record for most victories. Clayton's outstanding efforts earned him the Gatorade National Baseball Player of the Year. The pitching sensation beat out 459,000 other players for the amazing achievement!

"Without question, Clayton is deserving of recognition as the nation's best high school baseball player based on his performance and the tremendous ability he's demonstrated," said Gatorade Senior Vice President Tom Fox. "But he is also a shining example to peers and aspiring young players of what a leader and a student-athlete should be."

"Clayton has electric stuff on the mound," Highland Park head coach Lew Kennedy raved to *PRNewswire*. "He competes well and has a knack for getting strikeouts in tough situations. He is a humble young man who is a great role model for our team and community."

On graduation night, Highland Park High's senior class celebrated reaching a huge milestone in their life. Although Clayton, who graduated with an impressive 3.7 grade point average, took a few moments to enjoy his high school graduation, he silently mulled over his future. Unbeknownst to many people, the popular athlete had a weighty decision to make.

A&M University had offered him a full scholarship. In a stroke of good luck, Ellen had also been accepted to the college. Yet, several Major League Baseball teams had indicated their willingness to sign Clayton to a professional contract straight out of high school.

Would the pitching sensation choose college, or would he head straight to the big leagues?

Clayton & Ellen
Andrew Evans - PR Photos

"Wherever I go, it doesn't matter because I'm just going to pitch and see where they put me."

On June 6, 2006, Major League Baseball held their annual first-year player draft. In the eagerly-awaited event, each professional team drafts one player at a time over 50 rounds. Clayton waited anxiously all day to see which team would select him.

In the end, the Los Angeles Dodgers, who had watched Clayton for months, selected him in the first round. He was the seventh selection overall, and the youngest one, too. The historic Southern California team offered the eighteen-year-old a signing bonus worth $2.3 million! It was an offer too sweet to resist. The youngest Kershaw turned down his scholarship to Texas A&M and signed with the Dodgers.

"I'm excited for Clayton and his family that he is ready to sign and get his career started," Logan White, scouting director for the Dodgers, remarked to *Scout.com*. "I compare him to Dave Righetti. He throws from a high angle, has a power fastball, a good curveball and a feel for a changeup. He's got a natural delivery and he's a great makeup kid."

After signing Clayton to a professional contract, the Dodgers flew their newest player to Los Angeles for a special series of events. When the young pitcher arrived at Dodger Stadium, he looked around in awe. The historic ballpark had hosted many memorable moments over the years, like Kirk Gibson's 1988 World Series home run and Sandy Koufax's 1965 perfect game. Soon Clayton would take the mound and perhaps make his own history.

Later that year, Clayton traveled to Florida to begin his professional baseball career. As a member of minor league's Gulf Coast Dodgers, the teenager played in picturesque Vero Beach. In his first season, he delivered strong numbers, posting a 1.95 ERA and 54 strikeouts in 10 games.

One year later, Clayton earned a promotion to the Class AA league. Playing for the Jacksonville Suns, the pitching talent suddenly sat just two leagues away from the majors. He helped the Suns end the year with a second-place finish in the Southern League.

Although Clayton did not yet play under the intense big-league spotlight, he attracted considerable attention from baseball experts and fans. In fact, the prized prospect already drew comparisons to the Dodgers' most successful pitcher of all time, Hall of Famer Sandy Koufax. The two men shared several key resemblances. They were both lanky left-handers with a brilliant curveball, a mid-90's fastball and made an intimidating presence on the mound.

Koufax took a keen interest in the Dodgers' exciting phenom. Like many baseball fans, Clayton's enormous potential thrilled him. On one occasion, both men shared a private jet to a spring training game. During the 60-minute flight, the two talents spoke almost exclusively about pitching.

"We talked for an hour and it was unbelievable," Clayton told *USA Today*. "I learned more on one plane trip than I have in a long time."

Vero Beach, Florida
Joseph Dzidrums

Truth be told, though, comparisons to the legendary Koufax also made Clayton uneasy. He felt reluctant to shoulder such weighty expectations. The determined player wanted to carve his own career and create his own legacy.

"I'm not trying to be anybody else," he told the *Los Angeles Times*. "I've got expectations for myself to succeed that surpass anybody else's."

Entrance to Dodgertown
Joseph Dzidrums

Despite leading a bustling baseball life, Clayton maintained a strong relationship with his loved ones. The teenager kept in constant contact with longtime girlfriend Ellen, who attended Texas A&M as a communications major. He also phoned his mom regularly. For her part, Marianne kept her son's bedroom exactly as he left it with sports trophies, photos and high school memorabilia remaining untouched.

2008 was a momentous year in Clayton's life. After producing a solid spring training with the Dodgers, the twenty-year-old began the season back in Class AA baseball as a key member of the Jacksonville Suns. Many experts predicted the future superstar would be promoted to Class AAA ball by the end of the season. In 13 game appearances for the Suns, he produced a remarkable 1.91 ERA and struck out 59 batters.

One spring evening, the Suns were playing a series against the Mudcats in Zebulan, North Carolina. After a night game, Clayton stood in the locker room changing into his street clothes when someone tapped his shoulder. Manager John Shoemaker wanted to see the gifted hurler in his office as soon as possible.

As Clayton walked to Shoemaker's office, he hoped that he was being promoted to the Dodgers Class AAA team in Las Vegas, Nevada. Instead, the ballplayer received life-changing news.

"You're heading to Los Angeles," his manager informed him.

In just a few days, Clayton Kershaw would take the mound at historic Dodger Stadium for his Major League Baseball debut.

*"I never felt like a kid.
We're all peers up here.
This is a clubhouse full of
teammates. No one is a kid."*

Chapter Four

After hearing news of his big-league promotion, Clayton grabbed his cell phone and immediately called his mother in Texas. Marianne was heading into a high school basketball game when her phone rang.

"Buy plane tickets to Los Angeles," her son announced. "The Dodgers just called me up to the majors."

A thrilled Marianne spent the next few hours frantically booking a last-minute trip to Southern California. It felt surreal to know that she would soon be at Dodger Stadium watching her son pitch in the majors.

Most rookies enjoy quiet Major League Baseball debuts, but Clayton arrived in Los Angeles with great fanfare. Baseball experts had followed the phenom's progress for years. Upon entering the Dodgers' clubhouse, the left-handed pitcher looked around in disbelief. A feet away, heroes Nomar Garciaparra and Jason Schmidt, prepared for the game.

Ultimately, Clayton chose 22 for his uniform number. The selection was a nod to childhood hero Will Clark, who wore the number during his baseball career. In the meantime Dodger veterans couldn't resist having fun with the newcomer. Several players replaced Clayton's jersey with that of his idol, Jason Schmidt. For several minutes, the rookie roamed the field during pre-game batting practice unaware that he was wearing the wrong uniform. When a third party informed Clayton about the jersey prank, he laughed good-naturedly.

The following morning Clayton Kershaw awoke full of nerves and anticipation. In a few hours he would make his Major League debut. The Dodgers gave their prized prospect a welcome fit for a movie star. The team sent a limo to his hotel to drive him to Dodger Stadium.

Clayton arrived at Chavez Ravine four hours before the game's 1:10 start time. The rookie kept busy by surfing the Internet. He also reviewed signs with catcher Russell Martin and read scouting reports on the opposing players.

Twenty of Clayton's family and friends made the trip to Los Angeles. At one point, Ellen ran to DSW to purchase dress shoes for her boyfriend who needed them to adhere to his team's strict dress code.

Dodger Stadium
Joseph Dzidrums

Twilight at Chavez Ravine
Joseph Dzidrums

An hour before game time, excited fans shuffled into Dodger Stadium. Everyone anticipated a great game. The Boys in Blue would face their rivals the St. Louis Cardinals. Would the team's prized rookie flourish under the bright spotlight, or wilt under the pressure?

Baseball lovers learned the answer quickly when Clayton struck out the side in the first inning. Dodger fans roared for the heralded prospect's strong start. In the end, the young pitcher notched seven strikeouts over six innings. His strong effort helped the Dodgers cruise to a victory.

"A left-hander that throws 96 with a snapdragon curve-ball and nasty changeup? That's pretty good," Russell Martin told *Yahoo! Sports* after the game. "Not a lot of guys have that stuff in the majors."

The Big Leagues
PR Photos

Following the game, reporters crowded the Dodgers' locker room to interview baseball's new sensation. Ever a class act, Clayton spent a long time patiently fielding a multitude of questions. While the newcomer reflected on his debut, he clutched two souvenir balls, one represented his first strikeout and the other marked his first pitch. His expressive eyes sparkled with excitement and wonder.

"You can't really explain how it feels out there," he gushed. "You can't know how it feels. You just know you've reached the plateau of baseball, and it's a pretty good feeling."

Shortly after uttering those words, the hard-working player left the clubhouse. He had to meet his family and friends for a well-deserved celebratory dinner.

Major League Dugout
PR Photos

"Winning 20 games is special, winning it at home, winning it against the Giants is something I'll remember for a long time."

Chapter Five

Clayton Kershaw quickly became a regular fixture in the Los Angeles Dodgers' starting rotation. In the 2009 season, his steady pitching helped lead the popular team to the playoffs, where they won the National League Division Series but faltered in the next round. He emerged even stronger in 2010 by finishing the year with a winning record and a whopping 212 strikeouts.

Life off the baseball diamond was equally charmed. On December 4, 2010, Clayton Kershaw and Ellen Melson were married in Texas at Highland Park Presbyterian Church. Fittingly, the groom wore blue sneakers, and a "Welcome to Dodgertown" sign greeted guests at the wedding reception.

Although Texas would always be close to Clayton's heart, the Kershaws bought a beautiful home in Pasadena, California. They would live there primarily during the baseball season. In fact, the couple's new residence in the bustling, multi-cultural city was located just minutes away from Dodger Stadium.

2011 marked a momentous year for Clayton. The hurler began the season in grand fashion when he was chosen as the Dodger's Opening Day starter. Typically, the selection is reserved for a team's top pitcher. Needless to say, the young Texan had evolved into Los Angeles' pitching ace.

Midway through the season, Clayton achieved a childhood dream by earning a spot in Major League Baseball's prestigious All-Star game. His teammates included several baseball superstars, like Chipper Jones, Scott Rolen and fellow Dodger Matt Kemp. When Clayton took the mound for an inning, he didn't surrender any runs and even recorded a strikeout. Ultimately, his contribution helped the National League beat the American League, 5-1.

Following the All-Star break, Clayton dominated the remainder of the season. Showing a maturity beyond his years, the Dodgers' pitching ace amassed 21 wins, 248 strikeouts and a 2.28 ERA. The imposing statistics snagged him baseball's coveted triple crown. He became the first Dodger to accomplish the feat since Sandy Koufax in 1966.

On November 17, 2011, during end-of-the-season festivities, Clayton received baseball's highest pitching honor: the Cy Young Award. Voted on by the Baseball Writers Association of America, the award rewards the best pitcher in each league. Past recipients have included: Don Drysdale, Sandy Koufax, Greg Maddux and Roger Clemens.

Kershaw Prepares
Joseph Dzidrums

In the Stretch
Joseph Dzidrums

Moments after the announcement, Dodger broadcasting legend Vin Scully took the microphone at Chavez Ravine to introduce the winner to the press. The eloquent sportscaster had covered the team's games since 1950. Even so, the beloved icon, who had covered many baseball legends during his career, seemed mighty impressed with Clayton Kershaw.

"In his first year, in his first few games, it was as if he knew he belonged," Scully raved. "And he not only belonged, but in four years he has retained the heights of today, the Cy Young winner, and what a group he joins. Their pictures are here, and next year, his picture will be up as well. Ladies and Gentlemen, the Cy Young Award winner of 2011, the Los Angeles Dodgers left-handed pitcher Clayton Kershaw."

The Launch
Joseph Dzidrums

Press members in attendance burst into hearty applause for baseball's best pitcher. Flashbulbs flickered as photographers took Clayton's picture for their respective newspapers and websites. Ellen smiled proudly at her husband, while two high-profile Dodgers, Matt Kemp and James Loney, cheered enthusiastically for their teammate.

"Thank you all for coming, especially James and Matt, my teammates, it means a lot to me that you're here. I appreciate it," Clayton said. "First of all, I want to thank Ellen. She's been so special. It's my first year of marriage so it's been a good one.

"I want to thank my coaches, too. Rick Honeycutt has been awesome. The hard work that he's put in is so special that I'm really thankful for that.

"I want to thank Logan who drafted me and let me be a Dodger.

"I don't have a whole lot to say. The only thing I will say is I'm really humbled to be here. I always dreamed about playing baseball as a kid, maybe one day making it to the big leagues, but I never dreamed about anything like this. It really is special and I'm just really thankful for it."

When Clayton finished his warm speech, another rousing ovation greeted him. The kid from Texas had already heard plenty of applause over the years, and he was just getting started.

"I love LA.
I love being out here."

Chapter Six

Sports fans agreed that Clayton Kershaw had created waves on the field. Yet he began making a difference off the baseball diamond, too. A positive role model, the star often used his famous name to help others.

Ellen worked closely with Arise Africa, a Dallas-based non-profit organization that helps children improve their physical, economic and spiritual well-being. During the 2011 off-season, Clayton visited Zambia to meet children in need of help. After encountering an 11-year-old African girl named Hope, an HIV-positive double orphan, he began plans to build a Zambian orphanage. To achieve his lofty goal, he pledged to donate $100 for every strikeout he notched during the 2012 season. Ellen and Clayton also became Hope's personal sponsor.

In November of 2012, the Kershaws' orphanage, entitled Arise Home, officially opened its doors. At the festive grand opening, Clayton and Ellen joined Hope and seven other orphans at their new home. People danced, sang and prayed together at the joyous event. For the first time in their lives the children would sleep on beds every night. All who lived at Arise Home would also have sufficient food, shelter, clothing and an education.

"Ellen asked me what I wanted my legacy to be," Clayton told *MLB.com*. "You want to be remembered for something other than baseball. You can impact other people with your faith. That's the purpose of what this is all about."

Thanks to his noble efforts, in the fall of 2012, Clayton became the youngest player to win Major League Baseball's esteemed Roberto Clemente Award. The honor acknowledges the player who best represents the sport through meaningful contributions on and off the baseball diamond, including exemplary sportsmanship and community involvement.

Upon hearing the news, the unassuming player blinked back tears. He had never expected to be recognized so quickly. It felt humbling to join historic past recipients, such as Willie Mays, Cal Ripken, Jr. and Willie Stargell.

"The reaction was a little bit stunned, speechless," he admitted. "I didn't think I was going to win, so I wasn't really expecting it. To hear what it encompasses, it's pretty cool.

On Diamond Vision
Joseph Dzidrums

At the Supermarket

Christine Dzidrums

At the Plate
Joseph Dzidrums

"I've been fortunate to get to start playing baseball professionally at the big league level at an early age, and I'm so thankful for that. With that comes a great platform to do stuff off the field. I was just fortunate that I got a great start in L.A., and could start doing stuff off the field almost immediately."

"It's the most important award he could ever get, because it speaks about his character and his passion and his heart," Ellen told *MLB.com*. "It's amazing. It's such an honor. I don't know if anything can top this."

Although Clayton's charity work often made the news, quirky aspects of his family life inspired headlines, too. Word of the athlete's connection to a space legend came to light. He was the great nephew of Clyde Tombaugh, the famed astronomer who discovered the dwarf planet named Pluto.

Memorabilia
Joseph Dzidrums

"I know it sounds like a joke but it's true," Clayton laughed.

Tombaugh discovered Pluto on February 18, 1930, and it was officially designated as a major planet. However, on 2006 the International Astronomical Union (IAU) drafted new qualifications for planet classifications. Because Pluto only met two qualifications, it was downgraded to a dwarf planet. The celestial body's demotion sparked outrage from the general public. Soon science fans began sending the pitching sensation shirts declaring, "Pluto is still a planet!"

During his free time, Clayton enjoyed several relaxing activities. The doting husband often looked forward to date nights with Ellen. Sometimes he challenged family and friends to a game of ping pong, his second favorite sport.

Shortly after the start of the 2013 season, Christopher Kershaw passed away on Sunday, April 28. After learning the news, Clayton immediately flew home to be with family and attend his father's funeral. Ever the professional, he continued working out by throwing pitches on a Texas field with a high school catcher.

Chatting with A.J. Ellis
Joseph Dzidrums

Despite the personal tragedy, Clayton returned to Los Angeles five days after his dad's death. The focused player never missed a start in the Dodgers' pitching rotation.

"I was going to be back," Clayton told *The Associated Press*. "It was good to commemorate his life. But it was good to get back to baseball, too. It's weird watching games on TV."

"'Definitely a tough week but I had to do it," he added.

By Major League Baseball's 2013 season, Clayton Kershaw was no longer regarded as the promising upstart. Instead he was simply called the best pitcher in baseball. During that successful year, the superstar led the Dodgers to another division title. A few weeks later, he steered the team to victory in the Division Series of the playoffs. Sadly, in the next round against the St. Louis Cardinals, Los Angeles fell just short of making a World Series appearance. Despite the disappointment, baseball experts agreed that Clayton would one day pitch on baseball's largest stage. It was only a matter of time.

In the end, the dominant hurler finished the season with a league leading 1.83 ERA and 232 strikeouts. A month later, Clayton easily won his second Cy Young Award. He earned an impressive 29 of 30 first-place votes.

Not surprisingly, 2014 began with a bang for Clayton. He signed a seven-year contract with the Dodgers through the 2020 season. The $215 million deal was the largest contract for a pitcher in Major League Baseball history.

"It is an incredible privilege to be part of the Los Angeles Dodger organization for another seven years," Clayton remarked. "L.A. has become a second home to me and my wife, and I'm excited for the opportunity to represent the city for a long time to come. With this contract comes tremendous responsibility, not only as a pitcher, but as a good steward of the resources given to me. To whom much is given, much is required. Ellen and I are excited to take an undeserved blessing and, Lord willing, make a difference in the lives of others. I'm humbled by this recognition and looking forward to a new season, and hopefully, a World Series championship for the city of Los Angeles."

An L.A. Presence
Joseph Dzidrums

As a youngster living in Texas, Clayton Kershaw studied his baseball heroes and emulated their pitching mechanics. Sometimes he even fantasized about one day pitching in the big leagues. Today, young ballplayers all across the country now dream of becoming the next Clayton Kershaw.

No doubt about it, Clayton Edward Kershaw has become baseball's pitching ace.

On the Mound
Joseph Dzidrums

Essential Links

Clayton Kershaw's Official Twitter Account
https://twitter.com/ClaytonKersh22

Clayton Kershaw's Facebook Account
https://www.facebook.com/ClaytonKershaw22

Arise Africa
http://www.ariseafrica.org/arise-home

Kershaw's Challenge Official Page
http://www.kershawschallenge.com

Dodgers Official Web Site
http://dodgers.com

Official Major League Baseball Web Site
http://www.mlb.com

About the Author

Christine Dzidrums holds a bachelor's degree in Theater Arts from California State University, Fullerton. She has written biographies on many inspiring women: Joannie Rochette, Yuna Kim, Shawn Johnson, Nastia Liukin, The Fierce Five, Gabby Douglas, Sutton Foster, Kelly Clarkson, Idina Menzel and Missy Franklin.

Christine's first novel, *Cutters Don't Cry*, won a Moonbeam Children's Book Award. She also wrote the tween book *Fair Youth* and the beginning reader books *Future Presidents Club* and the *Princess Dessabelle* series.

Ms. Dzidrums lives in Southern California with her husband, three children and two dogs.

www.ChristineDzidrums.com
@ChristineWriter.

SportStars
They've Got Game!

    SportStars focuses on the world's most successful and influential athletes. ***Matt Kemp: True Blue Baseball Star*** tells the story of one of the Dodgers most successful players in history. ***Mike Trout: Baseball Sensation*** chronicles the New Jersey native's rise from a toddler running the base paths to winning the 2012 American League Rookie of the Year Award. A children's biography, ***66: The Yasiel Puig Story*** will help young readers learn about the man behind the baseball legend.

Build Your SkateStars™
Collection Today!

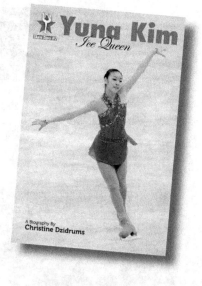

At the 2010 Vancouver Olympics, tragic circumstances thrust **Joannie Rochette** into the spotlight when her mother died two days before the ladies short program. Joannie then captured hearts everywhere by courageously skating two moving programs to win the Olympic bronze medal. *Joannie Rochette: Canadian Ice Princess* profiles the popular figure skater's moving journey.

Meet figure skating's biggest star: **Yuna Kim**. The Korean trailblazer produced two legendary performances at the 2010 Vancouver Olympic Games to win the gold medal. *Yuna Kim: Ice Queen* uncovers the compelling story of how the beloved figure skater overcame poor training conditions, various injuries and numerous other obstacles to become world and Olympic champion.

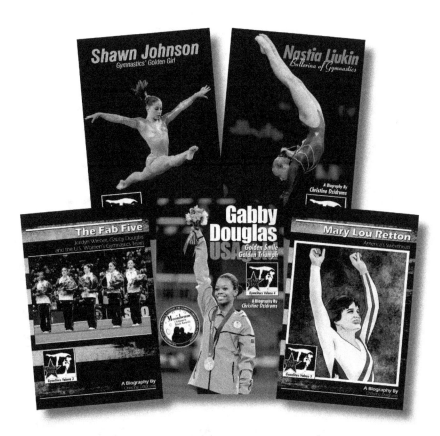
Now sports fans can learn about gymnastics' greatest stars! Americans **Shawn Johnson** and **Nastia Liukin** became the darlings of the 2008 Beijing Olympics when the fearless gymnasts collected 9 medals between them. Four years later at the 2012 London Olympics, America's **Fab Five** claimed gold in the team competition. A few days later, **Gabby Douglas** added another gold medal to her collection when she became the fourth American woman in history to win the Olympic all-around title. The *GymnStars* series reveals these gymnasts' long, arduous path to Olympic glory. *Gabby Douglas: Golden Smile, Golden Triumph* received a **2012 Moonbeam Children's Book Award**.

Our *YNot Girl* series chronicles the lives and careers of the world's most famous role models. *Jennie Finch: Softball Superstar* details the California native's journey from a shy youngster to softball's most famous face. In *Kelly Clarkson: Behind Her Hazel Eyes*, young readers will find inspiration reading about the superstar's rise from a broke waitress with big dreams to becoming one of the recording industry's top musical acts. *Missy Franklin: Swimming Sensation* narrates the Colorado native's transformation from a talented swimming toddler to queen of the pool.

Meet Timmy Martin, the world's biggest baseball fan.

One day the young boy gets invited to his cousin's birthday party. Only it's not just any old birthday party... It's a baseball birthday party!

Timmy and the Baseball Birthday Party is the first book in a series of stories featuring the world's most curious little boy!

Timmy Martin has always wanted a dog. Imagine his excitement when his mom and dad let him adopt a pet from the animal shelter. Will Timmy find the perfect dog? And will his new pet know how to play baseball?

Timmy Adopts A Girl Dog is the second story in the series about the world's most curious 4½ year old.

The SoCal Series

2010 Moonbeam Children's Book Award Winner! In a series of raw journal entries written to her absentee father, a teenager chronicles her penchant for self-harm, a serious struggle with depression and an inability to vocally express her feelings.

"I play the 'What If?'" game all the time. It's a cruel, wicked game."

When free spirit Kaylee suffers a devastating loss, her personality turns dark as she struggles with depression and unresolved anger. Can Kaylee repair her broken spirit, or will she remain a changed person?